Andrea Lyons © 2020

Ruby Green,
Hip-Hop Queen !

Written and Illustrated By
Andrea Lyons

Ruby Green is a
five
year old girl,
who loves to
dance !

© Andrea Lyons 2020.

When she was three,
her love of dance
began.

© Andrea Lyons 2020

By the time she was five,
she was Breakdancing
and Hip-Hopping
with talent and drive !

Andrea Lyons ©2020

She was Dancing Queen hot !
Skilled and stronger than not !
Ruby was Queen
of the Bainbridge Street Lot !

From Philadelphia , Pa.,to
Ventnor, New Jersey.
She was not lazy !
She outdanced her dog Sadie.
Now isn't that CRAZY ?

Ruby learned to do
Hip-Hop from watching her
brother.
Eli was older and faster, like
no other!
He was cool !
He was neat !
He was magic on his feet !

Andrea Lyons ©2020

As a team, Ruby thought,
she and Eli
Could not be beat !

Eli and Ruby go to Philly
Movemakers for Hip-Hop
Dance lessons.
Laurel their Dance teacher,
tells them to practice their moves
in their dance sessions.
They're getting ready for
an upcoming Dance show !
It's at The Performance Garage,
don't you know !

Eli and Ruby were in good
Shape !
Their hard work practicing
the moves paid off, and
they felt great !

The music in the show created a
feeling of happiness
so sweet,
as the children stepped to
the rhythm of the beat !
Freestyle and Breaking
the way
with the soles
of their feet !

Ruby and Eli's mom and dad
came to watch
with the whole family.
They were so proud !
They clapped their hands
and in front of the crowd,
called out to them,
"We love you Ruby and Eli ! "
Then the crowd howled
as Ruby and Eli bowed.

Andrea Lyons 2020©

This book is dedicated to Ruby and Eli Green,
and Jacob, Rebecca, and Charlie Mark.
It is written and illustrated by their Grandy,
Andrea Lyons.
July, 2020